I0839673

A B C in the SEA

Colouring Book

By Anita Gardner

ABC in the SEA is a beautifully illustrated colouring book
exploring the marvellous marine life on planet Earth.
Drawing in the reader to become an aquatic artist,
explorer and eco-hero.
To learn about the citizens of the sea but also how their lives
are intrinsic to our own. How our actions effect their
survival, and how their special powers enable ours to
continue.
ABC in the SEA colouring book welcomes the reader to
become the explorer in making their own mark on these
brilliant beings through their own creative experimentation
and expression, artistically, and in the life choices we make.
ABC in the SEA colouring book is available in digital and
traditional book format, as well as PDF format to be used as
an educational resource.
Either artistically developed using traditional art materials,
or coloured and edited using digital art programmes and
apps and shared with the Atelier Aquatic social media
community, thereby all over the planet!
ABC in the SEA provides a community canvas to add colour
to the magical marine world around you, and bring it to life
in your own world.

All profits from ABC in the SEA colouring book go to
Atelier Aquatic Community Interest Company,
Drawing inspiration from life in the Ocean to life on Earth.
Using art as a creative tool to engage communities in marine
conservation and positive change for citizens of the sea,
above and beneath the surface.
Art - Education - Marine Conservation.

www.atelieraquatic.org

This ABC in the SEA Colouring Book is designed to be
either printed as a PDF and coloured in with your
chosen art materials, eg: coloured pencil, markers, chalk
pastels, watercolour paint...
Or the more eco friendly choice;
use as a digital colouring book!

Take a screen shot of the page you want to colour on
your smart phone/tablet/computer, crop the image as
desired. Save and open with a drawing programme, eg;
Adobe programmes/apps, Sketchpad,
Pixlr Express, Paper 53...Save and share your artistic
masterpiece!
Create your ABC in the SEA masterpiece then save and
share on social media and the
Atelier Aquatic Community...
Drawing inspiration from life in the Ocean to life on Earth.

Atelieraquatic.org

 @AtelierAquatic

 @atelieraquatic

*With love and thanks to Reets for encouraging the artist in me,
and John for introducing me to the sea!*

A is for Anemone

A is for Anemone

* Anemones are a group of water-dwelling, predatory animals, they share the same name as the land based (terrestrial) flower.

* Anemones are beautifully coloured (reds, pinks, yellows) and look like flowers when the mouth, with tentacles, is fully open.

* Anemones are solitary polyps, unlike the closely related corals, these organisms do not have a skeleton.

* Anemones occur everywhere in the Oceans, at all depths, but are particularly abundant in coastal waters in coral reefs.

* Anemones are in the same family (phylum) as a Jellyfish, Anemone polyps lack the Medusa stage where they become free swimming like jellyfish.

* Anemones are predators, they immobilize their prey with the aid of specialized stinging cells called nematocysts.

* Anemones form symbiotic relationships with single-celled dinoflagellates, zooxanthellae or with green algae, zoochlorellae, that live within their cells.

* Anemones receive the carbon products of photosynthesis from Zooxanthellae. During the day Zoox gives Anemones up to 90% of the energy needed for metabolism, growth and reproduction.

* Anemones give Zoox nutrients, carbon dioxide, and an elevated position with access to sunshine.

* Anemones and Clown fish have a symbiotic mutualistic relationship, the clown fish feeds on small invertebrates that otherwise have potential to harm the sea anemone, and the poo from the clown fish provides nutrients to the sea anemone. The clown fish is protected from predators by the Anemone's stinging cells, to which the clown fish is immune. The clown fish emits a high pitched sound that deters butterfly fish, which would otherwise eat the anemone. Awesome!

Conservation Corner...

Our life as humans depends strongly on Anemones and coral reefs, over 1 billion people depend directly on reefs for their livelihood. Anemones and Coral reefs play a critical role in the carbon cycle of our planet, by taking calcium ions and dissolved carbon dioxide from the water and turning it into calcium carbonate forming their hard skeletons. This allows our oceans to become a sink for the carbon dioxide in the atmosphere.

Helping Humans...

Anemones and Coral reefs contribute over 30 billion dollars to the world economy each year. Anemones and Coral reefs help drive our weather and provide shoreline protection for human homes and cities, buffering areas from potentially damaging storms and ocean swells.

Action Stations...

Carbon emissions cause global warming. Global warming kill's coral reefs, we could choose sustainable food choices, for example the humble vegetable and plant based diets. Check out this mental doco, www.cowspiracy.com...cow farts and burps could destroy the planet!, what a way to go.

B is for Butterfly fish

B is for Butterfly fish

* Butterfly fish have approximately 120 different species.

* Butterfly fish live on the coral reefs of the Atlantic, Indian, and Pacific Oceans.

* Butterfly fish are territorial and live in different areas of coral on the reef. Their colourful markings on their bodies are so they can identify which family (or species) they are from.

* Butterfly fish are omnivore's (eat both meat and plants). They eat different types of algae and seaweed, worms, small crustaceans and zooplankton.

* Butterfly fish have black stripes across their eyes, and eye-like spots on the body, this serves to confuse the predators and allow them to escape.

* Butterfly fish live in coral reefs and eat coral polyps, so they eat their own home!

* Butterfly fish use their long, thin snouts in search of worms, and other small invertebrates to eat.

* Butterfly fish species travel in small schools, although many are solitary until they find a partner, with whom they mate for life.

* Butterfly fish can fade their bright colourful markings at night time to hide from predators. Bonkers!

Conservation Corner...

Due to climate changes and ocean pollution in the last couple of decades, number of coral reefs and the number of butterfly fish decreased drastically. This group of fish is on the list of endangered species.

Helping Humans...

Butterfly fish are known as "Indicator Species", some are corallivores, meaning they rely on the live tissue of living coral for their food. If the coral is under stress due to poor environmental conditions the coral is less nutritious for the Butterfly fish and they move elsewhere. This change is an indicator of deteriorating coral health.

Action Stations...

Butterfly fish are often taken from the sea for the Aquarium trade, if you have a pet choose a sustainable one.

C is for Cuttlefish

C is for Cuttlefish

 * Cuttlefish are cephalopods, not fish. The cephalopods (meaning 'head-footed'), are a group of molluscs; the Octopus, Squid and Cuttlefish.

 * Cuttlefish, along with most cephalopods, are the Ocean's most intelligent invertebrates (animals with no backbone).

 * Cuttlefish have well-developed heads, with large eyes and mouths that feature beak-like jaws.

 * Cuttlefish have eight 'arms' with suckers, encircling around their mouth which are used to manipulate prey, there are also two tentacles with flattened paddle-like tips, which can be rapidly extended and are used to catch prey.

 * Cuttlefish have green-blue blood and 3 hearts! Fancy a cuttle?!

 * Cuttlefish swim using the fin that passes around the body. They can also rapidly expel water and move quickly by 'jet-propulsion'.

 * Cuttlefish have an internal shell known as a cuttlebone, which is filled with gas and aids buoyancy; these shells are found washed ashore, and are often given to pet birds as a source of calcium and other minerals.

 * Cuttlefish are colour blind!

 * Cuttlefish have special cells in their skin called Chromatophores which means they can change colour and pattern in a flash, their camouflage is so good that it can take on a checker board pattern placed beneath it. Cool!

Conservation Corner... Cuttlefish are super special; ecologically, the carnivorous cuttlefish are important in marine food chains, preying upon small molluscs, crabs, shrimp, fish, and other cuttlefish, while being preyed upon by dolphins, sharks, fish, seals, and other cuttlefish.

Helping Humans... In addition to adding to the wonder of nature, they are important in behavioural and neurological research given their highly-developed nervous system, brain, and eyes. The cuttlebone of cuttlefish offer addition values, including use as a source of calcium for caged birds and used as moulds by jewellers and silversmiths for casting small objects.

Action Stations... Global warming has a devastating effect on Marine Eco systems. Reduce your carbon emissions by walking or riding a bicycle - pollution free!

D is for Dragonet

D is for Dragonet

- Dragonet is also called the Mandarin fish.

- Dragonets have bright colours that give warning of its toxicity.

- Dragonet do not have scales; instead it produces a stinky mucus that covers its body. This mucus smells bad and tastes bitter. This warns off potential predators.

- Dragonet species display sexual dimorphism; males are usually much bigger than females and are coloured and patterned differently from each other.

- Dragonet are benthic organisms, spending most of their time near the sandy bottoms.

- Dragonets feed entirely on benthic sources, primarily copepods, amphipods, and other small invertebrates living on blades of sea grass.

- Dragonet mating involves a ritualized dance routine at dusk.

- Dragonet spawning behaviour is divided into four distinctive stages: courtship display (dancing), pairing, ascending, and sexy time...the release of sperm and eggs.

- Dragonets fights can be very intense; when one male recognizes another male near its breeding site, it will rush toward it and bite at its rival's mouth. Dangerous!

Conservation Corner...

Dragonets live in the tropical waters and coral reefs of the Indo-Pacific Seas. Coral reefs are home to 25% of all marine life on the planet. 50 % have gone in the last 30 years. Coral reefs are threatened by: Climate change, destructive fishing practices, overfishing, careless tourism, pollution, sedimentation, and coral mining.

Helping Humans...

Dragonet's dusk time disco is centre stage for eco-tourists via the diving and snorkelling industry. Coral reefs have a global value of $9.9 trillion USD. The total net benefit per year for tourism and recreation account for $9.6 billion.

Action Stations...

Learn about the brilliance and importance of coral reefs by watching the documentary Chasing Coral, join the campaign, chasingcoral.com

E is for Epaulette shark

E is for Epaulette Shark

Exceptional Epaulette Shark...

* Epaulette shark is a species of long tailed carpet shark, found in shallow, tropical waters off Australia and New Guinea.

* Epaulette sharks get their name from the large, white-margined black spot behind each pectoral fin, which look a little bit like military epaulettes.

* Epaulette shark is a small species usually under 1m, has a slender body with a short head and broad, paddle-shaped paired fins.

* Epaulette sharks have noctural habits and hang out in shallow water on coral reefs or in tidal pools.

* Epaulette sharks have evolved to cope with low oxygen levels to survive in tidal pools at night time, by increasing the blood supply to its brain and shutting down non- essential neural functions!

* Epaulette sharks are also known as the walking shark. They often "walk" by wriggling their bodies and pushing with their paired fins.

* Epaulette sharks can walk away from danger from other sharks.

* Epaulette sharks walk in shallow water and reefs to feed on animals in rock pools, small benthic invertebrates and bony fishes.

* Epaulette sharks are oviparous, the females lay eggs like birds.

* Epaulette sharks spot below its pectoral fin looks like a big eye to predators, so it scares them off! Excellent!

Conservation Corner...
Sharks have been around for more than 400 million years. Sharks are both feared and revered, but are now in danger, victims of irresponsible and unsustainable fishing practices. A quarter of the world's sharks and rays are threatened with extinction, according to The IUCN Red List of Threatened Species, with ray species found to be at a higher risk than sharks. The findings are part of the first ever global analysis of these species carried out by the IUCN Shark Specialist Group.

Helping Humans...
Removing these key predators from the food chain has serious consequences for marine ecosystems, which in turn has repercussions for people everywhere. The shark tourism industry has more to offer a country, in terms of generating revenue, than the shark fishing industry in many parts of the world. In the past few years, dead sharks landed at fishing ports are sold for small amounts, tiny in comparison to the potential for shark tourism.

Action Stations...
Learn about the special sharks that live on planet Earth, get involved...www.sharktrust.org

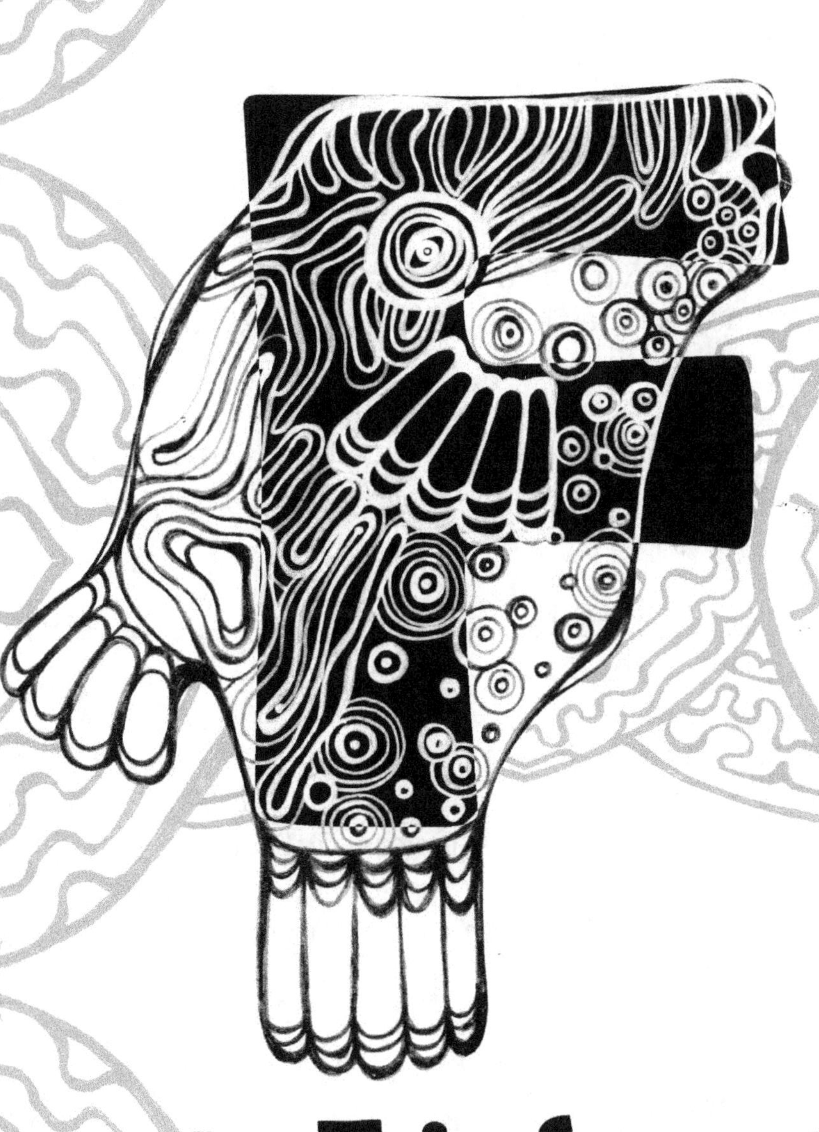

F is for
Fingerprint Toby

F is for Fingerprint Toby

Fascinating Fingerprint Toby...

* Fingerprint Toby is part of the puffer fish family.

* Fingerprint Toby is one of more than 120 species of puffer fish which live mostly in the warm waters of the Indian, Pacific and Atlantic Oceans, with only 30 species living in the freshwater.

* Fingerprint Toby body is covered in a toxic mucus, if they are eaten they can be fatal to humans, one fish contains enough toxin to kill 30 adult men!

* Fingerprint Toby meat is considered a delicacy in Japan (*fugu*), when prepared by specially trained chefs who know which part is safe to eat and in what quantity...risky!

* Fingerprint Toby's are not safe from sharks!, they are the only species immune to the fish's toxin.

* Fingerprint Toby can move their eyes independently, and many species can change the colour or intensity of their patterns in response to environmental changes. Just like the terrestrial chameleon.

* Fingerprint Toby are usually found in pairs on sandy bays or lagoon bottoms in the tropical West Pacific.

* Fingerprint Toby have bright colours and distinctive markings, although most puffers are a bit drab.

* Fingerprint Toby's body can suck up huge amounts of water (and air sometimes) to increase their body size and puff up like a football! Fab!

Conservation Corner...

Finger Print Toby live largely in the coral reefs of the world. Coral reefs can be found around the world and even in some places that you would not expect. In recent years scientists have discovered cold water coral reefs off the coast of Norway and deep underwater in the Mediterranean Sea. Coral reefs have survived tens of thousands of years of natural change, but many of them may not be able to survive the havoc wrought by humankind. Roughly 50% of coral reefs worldwide are already considered damaged beyond repair, with the other 50% under serious threat.

Helping Humans...

Tropical coral reefs are very productive ecosystems. Not only do they support enormous biodiversity, they are also of immense value to humankind. For many coastal societies around the world, coral reefs and their inhabitants are intricately woven into cultural traditions. Anyone who has floated with a mask and snorkel, immersed themselves in the three dimensional wonderland of a scuba dive, or experienced these habitats through media and books - a world without coral reefs would be an infinitely poorer place.

Action Stations...

Vote Earth by taking part in Earth Hour! As the biggest threat to coral reefs worldwide is climate change, we need to send a message to our leaders that warming must be limited to under 2 degrees Celsius.

G is for Grouper

G is for Grouper

* Groupers are the largest reef fish in the world, growing up to 3.5 metres long!

* Groupers are very slow swimmers, they rely on ambushing tactics to catch their prey. They eat lobsters, crabs, fish and even small sharks and young sea turtles, using their massive mouths to eat their prey whole.

* Groupers live in small groups, with one male and a harem of females. If the male grouper dies, one of the females is able to turn into a male and take over the harem!

* Groupers live in reefs throughout the Indian and Pacific Cceans, but they are considered vulnerable to extinction due to over-fishing.

* Groupers when young are yellow with black markings, but their colour changes to a duller green-Grey or brown when they get older. They can live for up to 50 years which is very old for a fish. Geriatric!

Conservation Corner...
While about 12 % of the land around the world is now under some form of protection (as national parks etc.), less than 4% of the ocean is protected in any way. Hope Spots allow us to plan for the future and look beyond current marine protected areas (MPA's), which are like national parks on land where exploitative uses like fishing and deep sea mining are restricted. Hope Spots are often areas that need new protection, but they can also be existing MPA's where more action is needed.

Helping Humans...
Hope spots; they can be large, they can be small, but they all provide hope due to:
- A special abundance or diversity of species, unusual or representative species, habitats or ecosystems
- Particular populations of rare, threatened or endemic species
- A site with potential to reverse damage from negative human impacts
- The presence of natural processes such as major migration corridors or spawning grounds
- Significant historical, cultural or spiritual values
- Particular economic importance to the community

Action Stations...
Get involved! support action groups, such as Mission Blue, www.mission-blue.org/act-now watch TED talk "Sylvia Earle: How to protect the Oceans (TED Prize winner!)"

H is for
Harlequin shrimp

H is for Handsome Harlequin Shrimp

Handsome Harlequin shrimp...

*   Harlequin shrimp are strong, they use their flat, oversize claws to sever arms from sea stars for food.

*   Harlequin shrimp only eat sea stars!

*   Harlequin shrimp have bright coloured bodies, which is thought to be warn off predators due to toxins in the bodies from eating sea stars.

*   Harlequin shrimp are monogamous, they stay in a pair for life.

*   Harlequin shrimp are the victims of bycatch. It is estimated that shrimp trawling, also known as "bulldozing the ocean," destroys 1.6kg of bycatch (unwanted seafood) for every 450g of shrimp taken. Horrible.

Conservation Corner...

For tens of millions of years, Earth's Oceans have maintained a relatively stable acidity level. It's within this steady environment that the rich and varied web of life in today's seas has arisen and flourished. But research shows that this ancient balance is being undone by a recent and rapid drop in surface pH that could have devastating global consequences. Since the beginning of the industrial revolution in the early 1800's, fossil fuel-powered machines have driven an unprecedented burst of human industry and advancement. The unfortunate consequence, however, has been the emission of billions of tons of carbon dioxide (CO2) and other greenhouse gases into Earth's atmosphere.

Helping Humans...

Scientists now know that about half of this anthropogenic, or man-made, CO2 has been absorbed over time by the Oceans. This has benefited us by slowing the climate change these emissions would have instigated if they had remained in the air. But relatively new research is finding that the introduction of massive amounts of CO2 into the seas is altering water chemistry and affecting the life cycles of many marine organisms, particularly those at the lower end of the food chain, shell forming animals such as Harlequin shrimp.

Action Stations...

Calculate your carbon print, www.carbonfootprint.com/calculator.aspx . Reduce your fossil fuel emissions and carbon footprint.

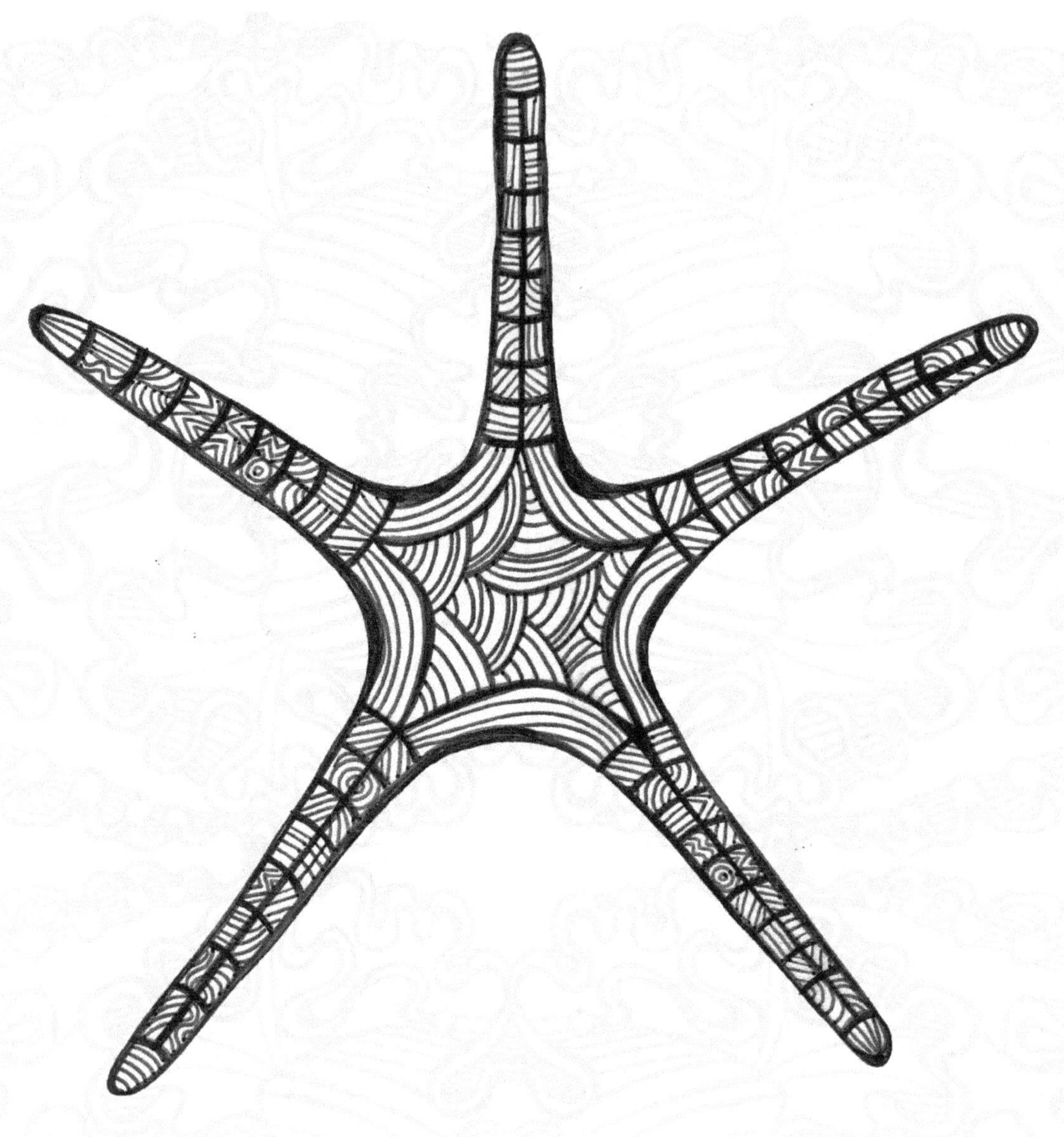

I is for Iconic Seastar

I is for Iconic Sea Star

Inspiring Iconic Sea Star...

* Iconic sea stars are star-shaped echinoderms, the common name given to any member of this animal kingdom, Greek translation *echinos* – "hedgehog" and *derma* – "skin". Echinoderms are also the largest phylum that has no freshwater or terrestrial (land-based) representatives, here are over 7000 species.
* Iconic sea stars are recognizable by their (usually five-point) radial symmetry, and are in the same family as sea urchins, sand dollars, sea cucumbers and brittle star.
* Iconic sea stars are one of the 1,500 species of sea star on the seabed in all the world's Oceans, from the tropics to frigid polar waters. They are found from the intertidal zone down to abyssal depths, 6,000 m below the surface.
* Iconic sea stars can produce sexually or asexually, this is where the central disc breaks into two pieces and each portion then regenerates the missing parts!
* Iconic sea star has cleverly evolved hydraulic tube feet connected to an elaborate water-vascular system that encircles the animal's mouth and extends via five radial canals down the centre of each arm.
* Iconic sea star's mouth is underneath, but their prey is absorbed outside their mouths by forcing out their digestive organs from their stomach.
* Iconic Sea Stars are carnivores and feed on almost any food including molluscs, worms, and each other!
* Iconic Sea Stars can be venomous.
* Iconic Sea Stars have special powers, when attacked and damaged by predators they are able to grow new arms! Ingenious!

Conservation Corner...

We create a lot of plastic... waste. And a lot of it ends up in the Oceans. All this plastic does not go away but builds up to create a gigantic "plastic ocean soup", in the Pacific it is up to 15 million square kilometers - almost the size of Russia. It's getting bigger, over the next 10 years, the plastic soup could double in size. At this speed, the plastic grows as much as 8 football fields every second. The plastic soup consists mainly of plastic bottles and caps, and, above all, plastic bags. A good argument for recycling and using bio-degradable bags. In the plastic soup there are 60 pounds of surface plastic to every one pound of plankton. Plankton is THE source of the food chain in the Ocean, affecting all marine life, including Iconic sea stars.

Helping Humans...

Plastic normally takes thousands of years to decompose. But 16-year-old Daniel Burd made it happen in just three months by isolating a microbe that lunches on plastic bags. Burd mixed landfill dirt with yeast and tap water, then added ground plastic and let it stew. The plastic indeed decomposed more quickly than it would in nature; after experimenting with different temperatures and configurations, Burd isolated the microbial munchers. One came from the bacterial genus *Pseudomonas*, and the other from the genus *Sphingomonas*. wwsef.uwaterloo.ca/archives/2008/08BurdReport.pdf

Action Stations...

Citizen Love wants to inspire you to think and live greener. They believe that shopping is political. How you spend your money says something about what you believe in, because your choices help to shape the world—and that makes a difference. So you've got to start somewhere, they would like you to support this simple choice: No more plastic bags! The fastest way to stop using plastic bags is to start carrying reusable bags—every day, all the time. They have collaborated with Plastic Artist, Dianna Cohen, to create a green bag design. They're made from recycled cotton (the waste scraps that normally go straight to landfill) and PET (which is made from plastic bottles). They reduce landfill and waste, they look stylish, and, most importantly, they replace the 700-1,000 bags the average family discards every year, www.citizenlove.com

J is for
Jolly Green Giant

J is for Jolly Green Giant

Jubilant Jolly Green Giant...

* Jolly green giants are one of more than 3,000 known species of Nudibranch, and new ones are being identified almost daily! Also known as sea slugs.

* Jolly green giants are found throughout the world's Oceans, but are most abundant in shallow, tropical waters.

* Jolly green giant's scientific name, Nudibranchia, means "naked gills", and describes the feathery gills and horns that most wear on their backs.

* Jolly green giant's brilliant colour and pattern can in itself act as a deterrent against predators.

* Jolly green giants are benthic animals, found crawling over the substrate on the ocean floor. The only exceptions to this are the Glaucus, or *blue dragon* nudibranch, which float upside down just under the ocean's surface.

* Jolly green giants sing! Nudibranch have been found to emit sounds that are audible to humans.

* Jolly green giants and all nudibranchs are hermaphrodites, they have a set of reproductive organs for both sexes, but they cannot fertilize themselves. Nudibranchs typically deposit their eggs within a gelatinous spiral.

* Jolly green giants are carnivores that graze on sponges, anemones, corals, barnacles, and even other nudibranchs, they get their colour from the food they eat, which helps in camouflage!

* Jolly green giants are solar powered sea slugs! Some Sacoglossans (type of sea slug) simply digest the fluid which they suck from the algae, but in some other species the slugs sequester and utilize within their own tissues the living chloroplasts from the algae they eat, a very unusual phenomenon known as kleptoplasty, for the "stolen" plastids. This earns them the title of the "solar-powered sea slugs", Juicy!

Conservation

Jolly green giant and many other nudibranch live in coral reefs and are an important part of that Eco system. Major threats to coral reefs and their habitats including pollution, urban and industrial waste, sewage, agrochemicals, and oil pollution are poisoning reefs. These toxins are dumped directly into the ocean or carried by river systems from sources upstream. Some pollutants, such as sewage and run-off from farming, (such as fertilizers or chemicals used in animal agriculture) increase the level of nitrogen in seawater. This causes an overgrowth of algae, which 'smothers' reefs by cutting off their sunlight, thereby stopping photosynthesis, on which many coral reefs and species rely on. One of which being the Jolly green giant.

Helping Humans...

Coastal protection is provided by coral reefs, they break the power of the waves during storms, hurricanes, typhoons, and even tsunamis. They help to prevent coastal erosion, flooding, and loss of property on the shore, the reefs save billions of dollars each year in terms of reduced insurance and reconstruction costs and reduced need to build costly coastal defences, not to mention the reduced human cost of destruction and displacement.

Action Stations...

Support a marine conservation charity, such as the Marine Conservation Charity, get involved; donate, volunteer, fund-raise, www.mcsuk.org

K is for
Knobbly Perriwinkle

K is for Knobbly Periwinkle

Knowledgeable Knobbly Periwinkle...

* Knobbly Periwinkle is a robust inter-tidal species with a dark knobbly shell. It is native to the rocky shores of the North Atlantic Ocean.

* Knobbly Periwinkle are part of the Gastropods family, known as snails and slugs, all kinds and all sizes from microscopic to large.

* Knobby Periwinkle texture helps to keep these snail cool when out of water and so they are able to survive for weeks without being immersed in water.

* Knobbly Periwinkles can breathe air so they can be seen on the rocks above the high tide line.

* Knobbly Periwinkles look like rocks but they do move! But only at high tide or in cool weather.

* Knobbly Periwinkles need to stay on the rocks, if they are taken off they will wash away with the tide and may die.

* Knobbly Periwinkles are eaten all over the shores of the Atlantic including England. The name 'periwinkle' comes from the Old English for 'penny winkle' as they were then sold for a penny per handful.

* Knobbly Periwinkles can live up to 20 years old! King-size!

Conservation Corner...

Plastic can smother and suffocate coastal marine life. More than 8 million tons of plastic is dumped into our oceans every year. Plastic is cheap and incredibly versatile with properties that make it ideal for many applications. However, these qualities have also resulted in it becoming an environmental issue. We have developed a "disposable" lifestyle and estimates are that around 50% of plastic is used just once and thrown away. Plastic is a valuable resource and plastic pollution is an unnecessary and unsustainable waste of that resource.

Helping Humans...

Oceans are fundamental to the health of our planet. The life blood of Earth's eco system. To survive and prosper mankind needs to harmonise its relationship with the planets Oceans. 50-85% of the oxygen we breath is produced by marine plants. 97% of the Earth's water supply is contained in the ocean. 30% of CO2 emissions produced by humans are absorbed by the Oceans.

Action Stations...

Plastic ponder...use reusable cups and bottles. The US Consumes 1500 Plastic water bottles every second. Stop using plastic straws, 550 million are thrown away in the UK and USA everyday. Use reusable bags, not plastic. 1 Trillion plastic bags discarded worldwide every year. See Atelier Aquatic resources page for plastic infographic downloads, www.atelieraquatic.org/resources

L is for Lancet fish

L is for Lancet fish

Lively Lancet fish...

* Lancet fish are large oceanic predatory fish.

* Lancet fish grow up to 2 metres in length!

* Lancet fish inhabits all the oceans of the world except the Polar Regions.

* Lancet fish often get caught on fishing nets as by-catch.

* Lancet fishes Greek name translates to "without scale lizard"

* Lancet fish feed mainly upon planktonic crustaceans, squids and salps (a palegic invertebrate related to the tunicate) and small fish.

* Lancet fish have also been known to be cannibalistic, leading to the nickname of "cannibal fish".

* Lancet fish is believed to be an ambush predator, its narrow body and silvery colour would provide a good cover before attack!

* Lancet has a large mouth and sharp teeth it can engulf the prey before it would have the chance to escape!

* Lancet fish is a mystery of the sea, very little is known about its biology. Life!

Conservation Corner...

Lancet fish are pelagic fish, meaning they live and feed in the open water. The North Pacific Subtropical Gyre, located in the northern Pacific Ocean, is one of the five major oceanic gyres. This gyre covers most of the Norther Pacific Ocean. It is the largest ecosystem on Earth, located between the equator and 50 degress N latitude, and comprising 20 million square kilometers. The gyre has a clockwise circular pattern and is formed by four prevailing ocean currents: the North Pacific current to the north, the California Current to the East, the North equatorial current South, and the Kuroshio Current to the west. It is the site of an unusually intense collection of man-made marine debris, known as the Great Pacific Garbage Patch.

Helping Humans...

A 2017 study conducted by scientists from the University of California, and the University of Georgia concluded that of the 9.1 billion tons of plastic produced since 1950, close to 7 billion tons are no longer in use.The authors estimate that only 9 percent got recycled over the years, while another 12 percent was incinerated, leaving 5.5 billion tons of plastic waste to litter the oceans or land.

Action Stations...

Many personal care products like scrubs and peels now contain plastic particles. So, every time we exfoliate or peel off those dead cells, as the products are rinsed off, they go down the drain and that means we are flushing plastic into our seas where it contributes to the 'plastic soup' problem. Use the Good Scrub Guide by Flora and Fauna;
www.fauna-flora.org/initiatives/the-good-scrub-guide

M is for Manta ray

M is for Manta ray

Magnificent Manta ray...

*   Manta ray is so called because they were caught using a blanket-shaped trap called a Manta in Spanish.
*   Manta rays are slow-growing, large-bodied migratory animals with small populations sparsely distributed across the tropics of the world.
*   Manta rays are characterized by their large diamond-shaped body with elongated wing-like pectoral fins, ventrally placed gill slits, laterally placed eyes, wide terminal mouths, and paired cephalic lobes.
*   Manta rays have among the lowest reproductive rate of all elasmobranchs (a subclass of cartilaginous fish), typically giving birth to only one pup every two to three years after reaching maturity at approx.10 years. Gestation is thought to last 10 to 14 months.
*   Manta rays are pelagic planktivores, (open sea plankton eaters) thought to be a seasonal visitor along coastlines with regular upwelling.
*   Manta ray's largest species is the Giant Manta ray, whose central disc can measure up to 9 meters wide.
*   Manta rays possess gills in the lower body, through which it obtains oxygen from water.
*   Manta rays have the largest brain of all fish.
*   Manta rays will often visit "cleaning stations" where some fish species are responsible for removing parasites from their skin.
*   Manta rays are currently on Appendix II of Convention of international Trade of Endangered Species of Flora, lists that are threatened with extinction unless trade is closely controlled.
*   Manta rays are classified as "vulnerable" in the Red List of the International Union for Conservation of Nature. Miserable.

Conservation Corner...

A group of international conservation organizations launched a new strategy to combat the decline of sharks and closely related rays, while warning that the rays are even more threatened and less protected than the higher profile sharks, "Global Priorities for Conserving Sharks and Rays: A 2015-2025 Strategy".

Helping Humans...

WWF, Project AWARE and The Manta Trust have joined together to bring the world's first Responsible Shark & Ray Tourism: A Guide to Best Practice. Shark and ray tourism is on the rise globally. If current trends continue, the number of shark related tourism sites could more than double over the next twenty years. The Guide, developed in collaboration with science and industry, aims to create well managed shark and ray tourism operations, conserve species and benefit local communities.

Action Stations...

Get involved with www.mantatrust.org

N is for Napoleon Wrasse

N is for Napoleon Wrasse

Noble Napoleon Wrasse...

* Napoleon wrasse can grow up to 2m and up to 190kg in weight.
* Napoleon wrasse is a protogynous hermaphrodite. In other words, a female that changes into a male. There are actually two types of male wrasse: initial phase males and terminal phase males. They are born either as 'initial phase males' or females. At around 9 years old, some of the females turn into initial phase males. It is not known what prompts this change. Some initial phase males then go on to become terminal phase males.
* Napoleon wrasse gather together in large mating groups which comprise both males and females. There can be over 100 hump head wrasses in these groups. Pairs form within the group, and mating commences. Mating involves males fertilizing eggs that the female has released into the water.
* Napoleon wrasse can live a long time. Females can live to around 50 years, reaching sexual maturity at 5 to 7 years old.
· Napoleon wrasse is one of the most valuable fish in the live reef fish trade, and the rarity of this species leads to higher demand and prices of up to US$250-300/kg in China.
* Napoleon wrasse's diet consists of molluscs, fish, echinoderms (star fish, sea urchins, etc.) and crustaceans.
* Napoleon wrasse has been identified by scientists as being an 'umbrella species', playing an important part in a local ecosystem.
* Napoleon wrasse are classified as "Endangered " in the Red List of the International Union for Conservation of Nature. It is also considered to be 'conservation dependent', meaning that its survival is currently dependent on human intervention.
* Napoleon wrasse are on Appendix II of CITES, Convention of International Trade Endangered Species.
* Napoleon wrasse is a WWF priority species. WWF treats priority species as one of the most ecologically, economically and/or culturally important species on our planet. Newsflash!

Conservation Corner...

The main threat to the Napoleon wrasse is over-fishing. The species is much sought after, particularly as a live export for the restaurant industry. One way of catching the Napoleon wrasse alive is to stun it with cyanide or a similar poisonous substance. The poison is sprayed into the fishes habitat. The fish is forced to hide in a crevice or hole in the coral and becomes sluggish as the poison takes hold. The fisherman can then easily capture the fish, even breaking away parts of the coral reef in order to reach it. The fish is taken from the sea and put into a tank containing clean water. Here it recovers, ready to be transported and sold. The Napoleon wrasse is specifically targeted in this manner, and is harvested intensively. Because the fish takes several years to reach sexual maturity, intensive fishing can have a devastating effect on the population. Sadly, the Napoleon wrasse is a sought-after commodity. As the species becomes scarcer, its value rises proportionally.

Helping Humans...

Napoleon wrasse's diet includes several toxic species, such as sea hares, boxfish and the crown-of-thorns starfish — a species that is known to destroy coral reefs.

Action Stations...

Do not support the Live Reef Food Fish Trade, by not eating live fish at home or on holiday.

O is for Ocotopus

O is for Octopus

Outrageous Octopus...

* Octopus the word, is derived from a Greek language and it means eight-footed.
* Octopuses are soft-bodied, eight-armed molluscs, the same family as clams and snails.
* Octopus have 300 species and they are in the Cephalopod family along with squid, cuttlefish and nautilus
* Octopus, like other cephalopods have bilaterally symmetric with two eyes and a beak, with its mouth at the centre point of the arms (which are sometimes mistakenly called "tentacles") . The only hard structure in their body is the beak which looks like a parrot beak! They use their beaks for eating.
* Octopus, even a 50-pounder, can squeeze through a hole only 2 inches in diameter (basically, if their beak fits, they can get through). Octopus are about 90-percent muscle, they make excellent escape artists, like the infamous "Inky".
* Octopuses trail their eight arms behind them as they swim. They have two siphon's (tubes on their head) which are used both for breathing and for jet propulsion!
* Octopuses have a complex nervous system and excellent sight, are the most intelligent and behaviourally diverse of all invertebrates.
* Octopuses are the first invertebrates to be seen using tools, such as using a coconut shell to hide from potential predators and using rocks and jets of water as a tool.
* Octopuses can solve puzzles, distinguish shapes and patterns. They can develop both short- and long-term memory. They have been seen to play with a toy and to have individual responses and personalities.
* Octopuses can change their colour and texture of their skin to blend with their environment and become invisible!
* Octopuses inhabit various regions of the Ocean, including coral reefs, pelagic waters, and the seabed; some live in the intertidal zone and others at abyssal depths.
* Octopuses grow fast, mature early and are short-lived.
* Octopuses reproduce only once in their life, during breeding, the male uses a specially adapted arm to deliver a bundle of sperm directly into the female's mantle cavity, after which he becomes weak and dies.
* Octopuses are the most dedicated mama's. The female deposits fertilized eggs in a den, she will not eat for 3 months whilst caring for her young until they hatch, after which she dies of starvation.
* Octopuses defend themselves against predators by the expulsion of ink, the use of camouflage and threat displays, their ability to jet quickly through the water, and their ability to hide.
* Octopuses are all venomous, but only the blue-ringed octopuses are known to be deadly to humans, their poison can kill 30 humans!
* Octopuses vary in size and colour depending on their environment. Those that live in colder water will be much larger than those that live in tropical (warm) water.
* Octopuses use strong suction cups (240 on each arm), they hunt crabs, molluscs and crayfish.
* Octopuses have three hearts, nine brains, and blue blood. Two hearts pump blood to the gills, while a third circulates to the rest of the body. The nervous system includes a central brain and a smaller brain at the base of each arm which controls movement.
* Octopuses blood contains the copper-rich protein hemocyanin, which is more efficient than hemoglobin for oxygen transport at very low temperatures and low oxygen concentrations. Outstanding!

Conservation Corner... The main environmental threats to the Octopus are related to the destruction of its habitat or a reduction in its main diet of molluscs, crayfish, and crabs through excessive fishing or marine pollution.

Helping Humans... Octopuses have much to teach humans on adaptation and sustainability. They are the masters of change.

Action Stations... Think twice about ordering Octopus on the menu. You will be eating a very intelligent teacher.

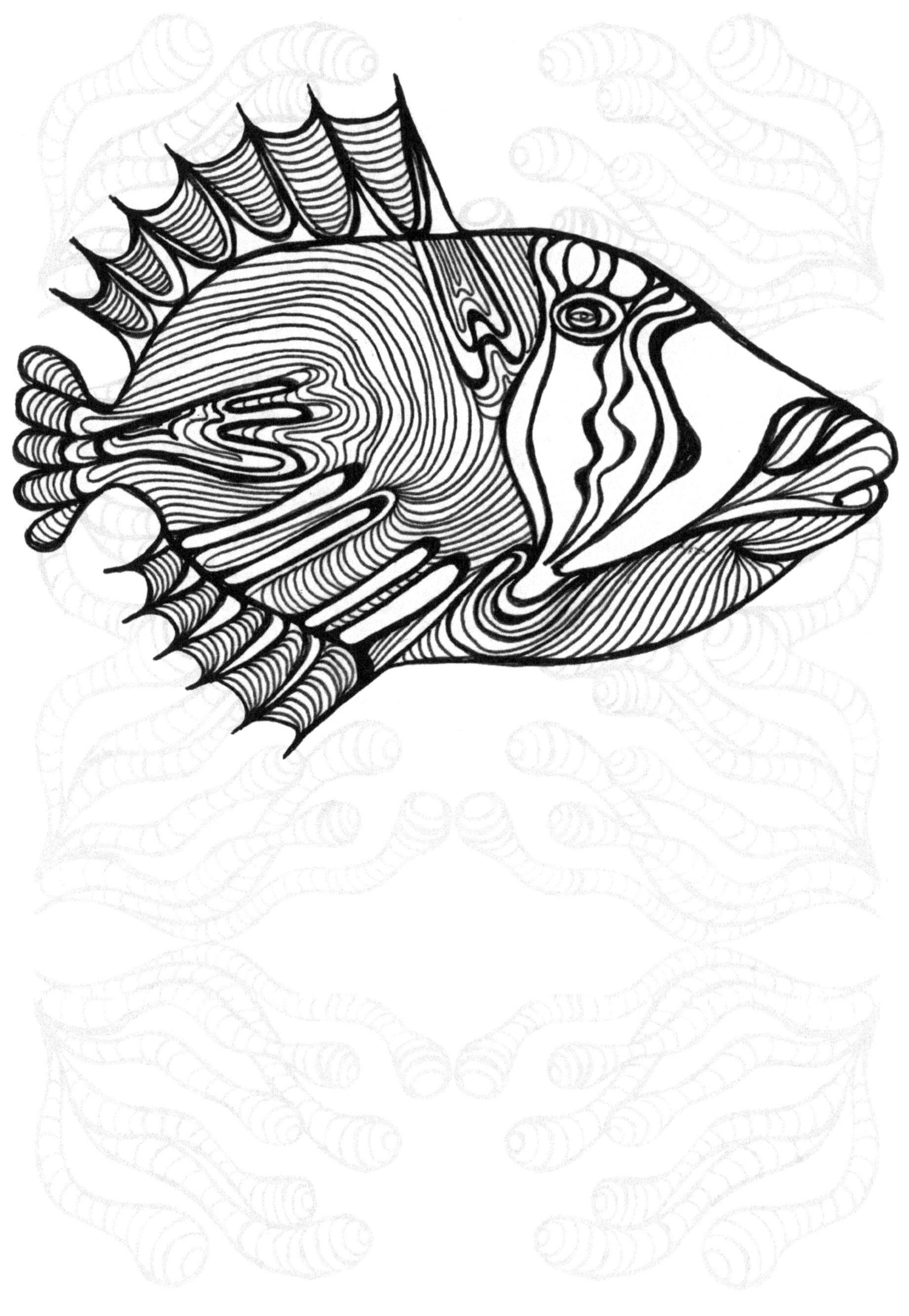

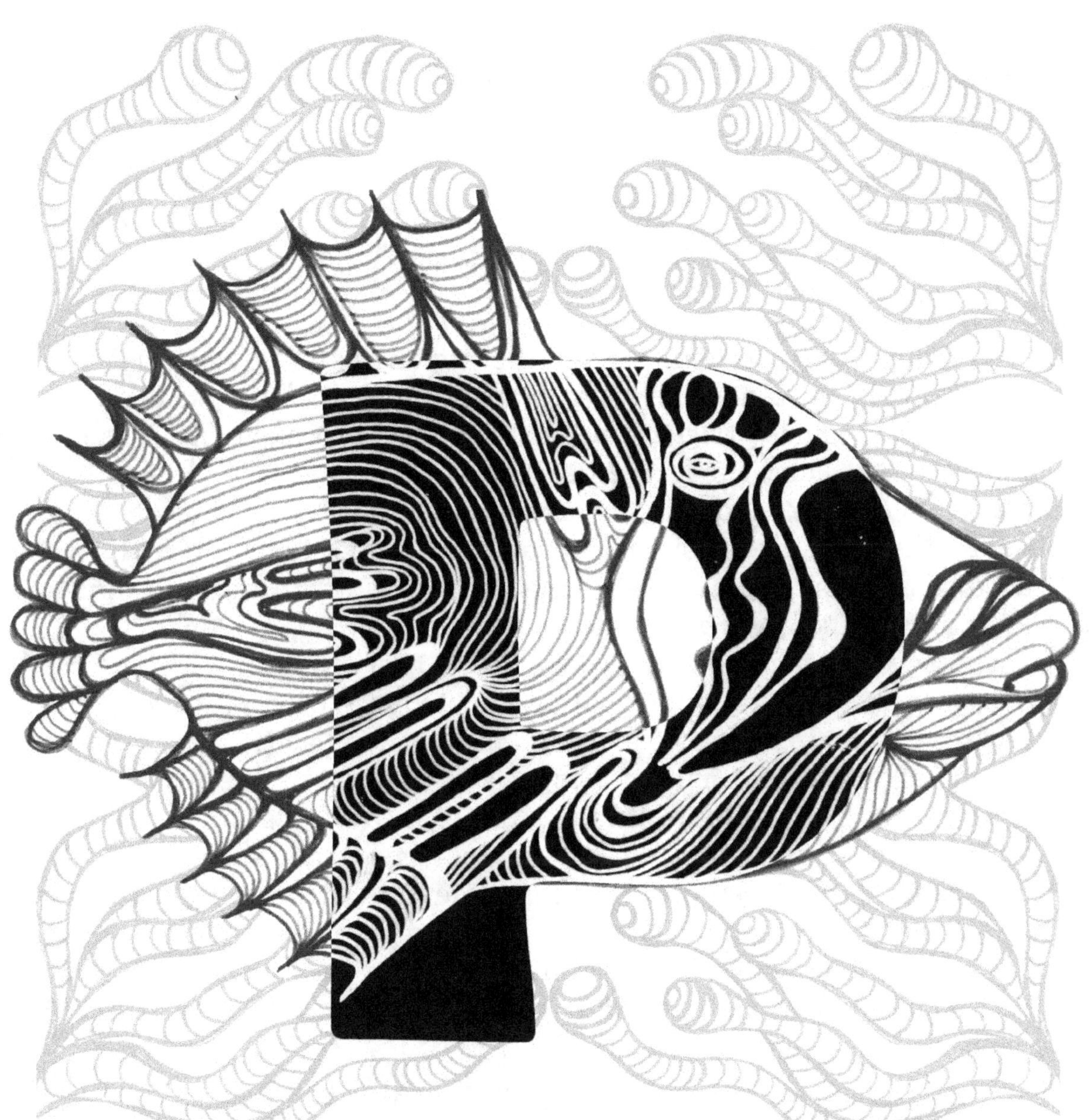

P is for Picasso fish

P is for Picasso Trigger Fish

Positive Picasso Trigger fish...

* Picasso trigger fish are named after the famous painter, Pablo Picasso, like his paintings they have a colourful appearance and striking patterns.

* Picasso trigger fishes "trigger" comes from the arrangement of their two dorsal spines: The larger spine can be locked or released by the smaller one (the trigger). This spine-locking mechanism allows trigger fishes to lodge themselves firmly in crevices where predators cannot harm or remove them.

* Picasso trigger fish is Hawaii's official state fish. It's Hawaiian name, *humuhumunukunukuapua'a*, means "nose like a pig."

* Picasso trigger fish can swim backwards and forwards.

* Picasso trigger fish live in tropical and subtropical oceans throughout the world, with the greatest species richness in the Indo-Pacific. Most are found in relatively shallow, coastal habitats, especially at coral reefs.

* Picasso trigger fish exhibit a level of intelligence that is unusual among fishes, and have the ability to learn from previous experiences.

* Picasso and Titan trigger fish viciously defend their nests against intruders, including scuba divers and snorkellers. Their territory extends in a cone from the nest toward the surface, so swimming upwards can put a diver further into the fishes' territory; a horizontal swim away from the nest site is best when confronted by an angry trigger fish!

* Picasso trigger fish , perform certain pre-spawning behaviours: blowing and touching. A male and female blow water on the sandy bottom (usually in the same spot at the same time) and set up their egg site. They touch their abdomens on the bottom as if they are spawning.

* Picasso trigger fish after spawning, both the male and female participate in caring for the fertilized eggs (bi parental egg care). The female blows oxygen over the eggs to help them hatch and the male guards the eggs from above.

* Picasso Trigger fish are very territorial some holding territory for eight years or longer. Protective!

Conservation Corner...

Picasso trigger fish live mostly in coral reefs, these are threatened by chemical run off from animal agriculture and intensive farming practices. Excess nutrients that run off land or are piped as wastewater into rivers and coasts can stimulate an overgrowth of algae, which then sinks and decomposes in the water. The decomposition process consumes oxygen and depletes the supply available to healthy marine life. Dead zones occur in many areas of the USA, particularly along the East Coast, the Gulf of Mexico, and the Great Lakes, but there is no part of the country or the world that is immune. The second largest dead zone in the world is in the USA, in the northern Gulf of Mexico.

Helping Humans...

Barack Obama has created the world's largest marine protected area by expanding an existing ocean reserve off Hawaii to cover 582,578 square miles, providing the final chapter in the president's conservation legacy. Conservationists discovered new species and importation ecological connectivity in the area, as well as raised concerns for the ecosystem due to the impact of ocean acidification and coral decline driven by warming temperatures.

Action Stations...

Research local Marine Protected Areas, find out more, how can you help? check out WWF MPA online for more info.

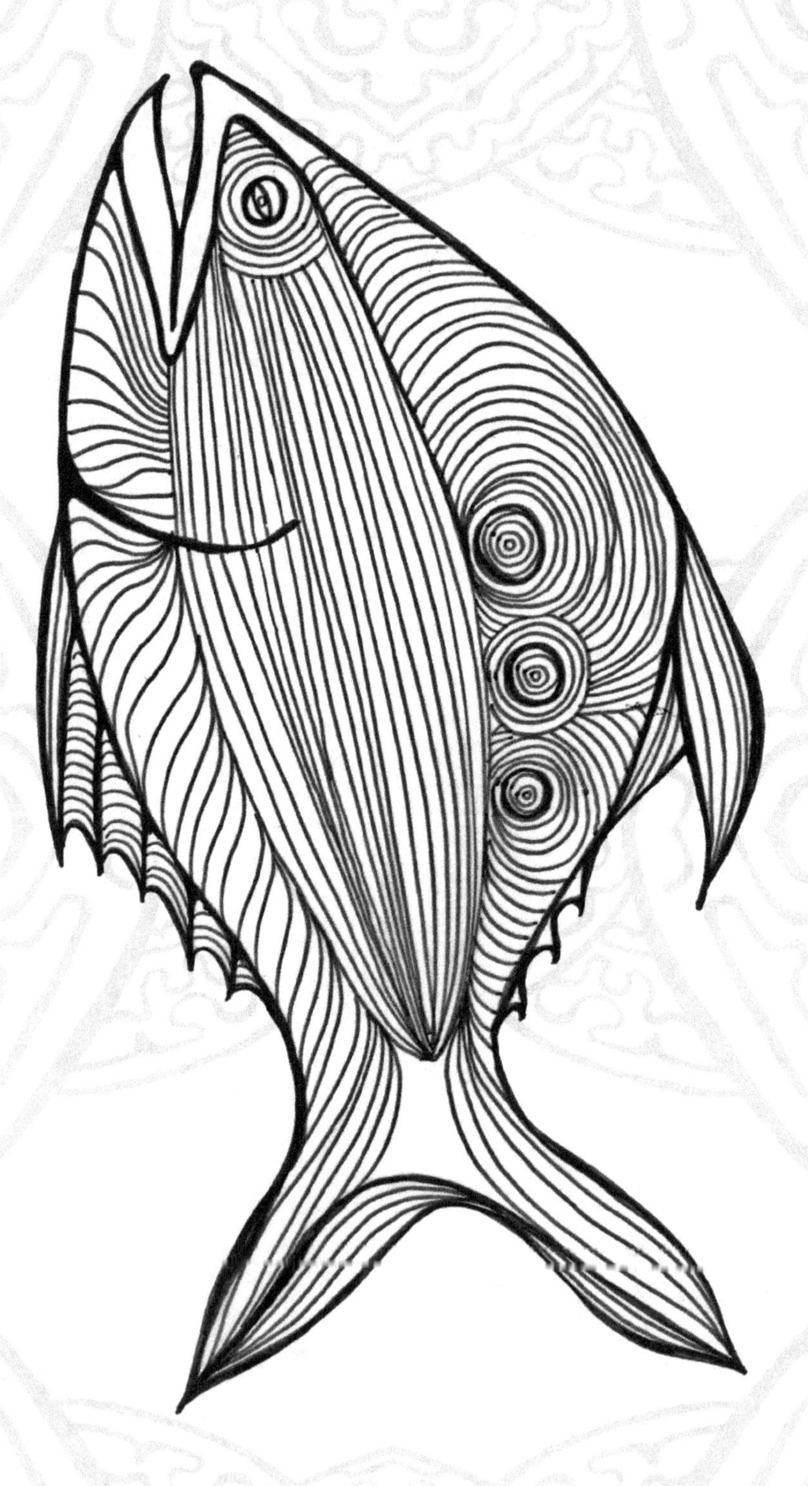

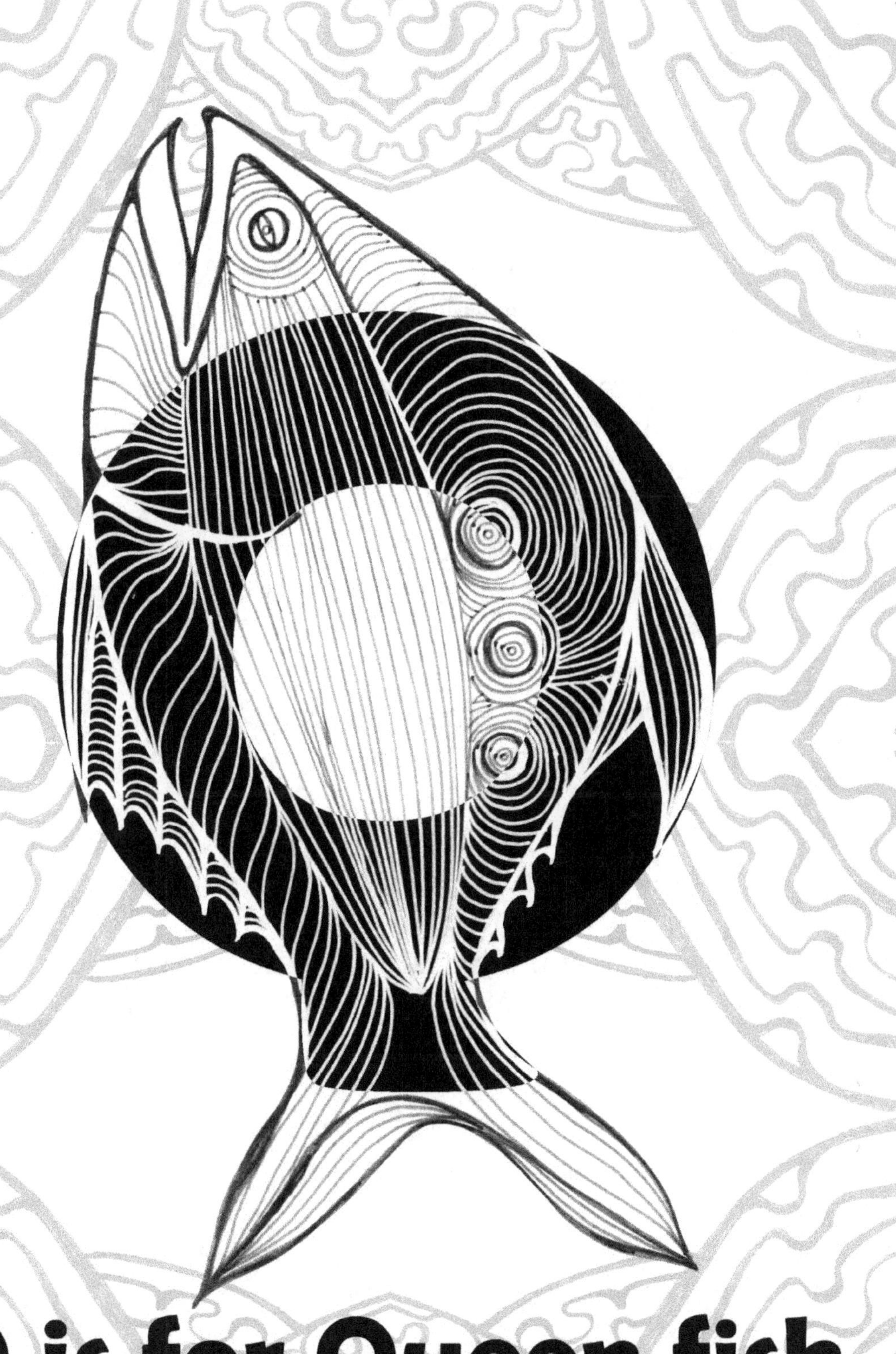

Q is for Queen fish

Q is for Queen-fish

Quality Queen-fish…

* Queen fishes nickname is "Queenie"! other names are leather skin, skinny fish, and giant dart.

* Queen fish are found in the Indo Pacific, Thailand, Okinawa, Indonesia, the Philippines, Papua New Guinea, Australia, and the east coast of Africa.

* Queen-fish are daytime feeders and prefer small pelagic fish, squids, and other fast moving prey, occasionally they may also feed on crustaceans.

* Queen-fish have a jutting lower jaw, large mouth and eyes. They have silvery bodies with rough skin.

* Queen-fish are a member of croaker family, so called due to the repetitive throbbing or drumming sounds they make!

* Queen-fish are a coastal species that can be found in offshore reefs, estuary systems, inshore reefs, rocky headlands, islands and bays.

* Queen-fish are extremely popular with sport fisherman, as they like the fight they put up when caught.

* Queen-fish are known for their speed, acrobatics, powerful agility and voracious appetites. Quintessential!

Conservation Corner... A study published in the journal Science estimated that one-third of global fisheries are in a state of collapse. Without more concerted efforts to reduce overfishing, pollution and marine habitat loss, the study researchers predicted that the seas will be totally drained of seafood as early as 2050.

Helping Humans... A plant-based diet (a.k.a vegan) cuts your carbon footprint by 50%

Action Stations... Take the 30 days vegan challenge, www.cowspiracy.com/take-action

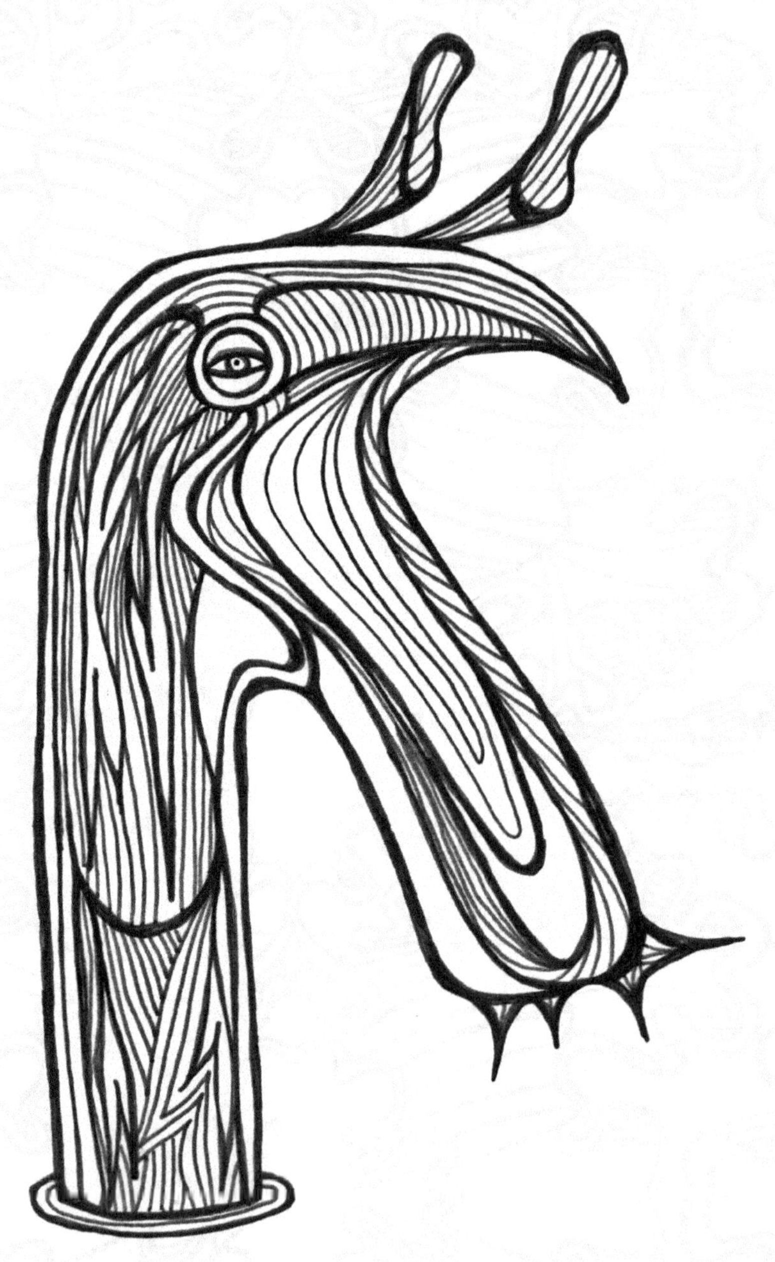

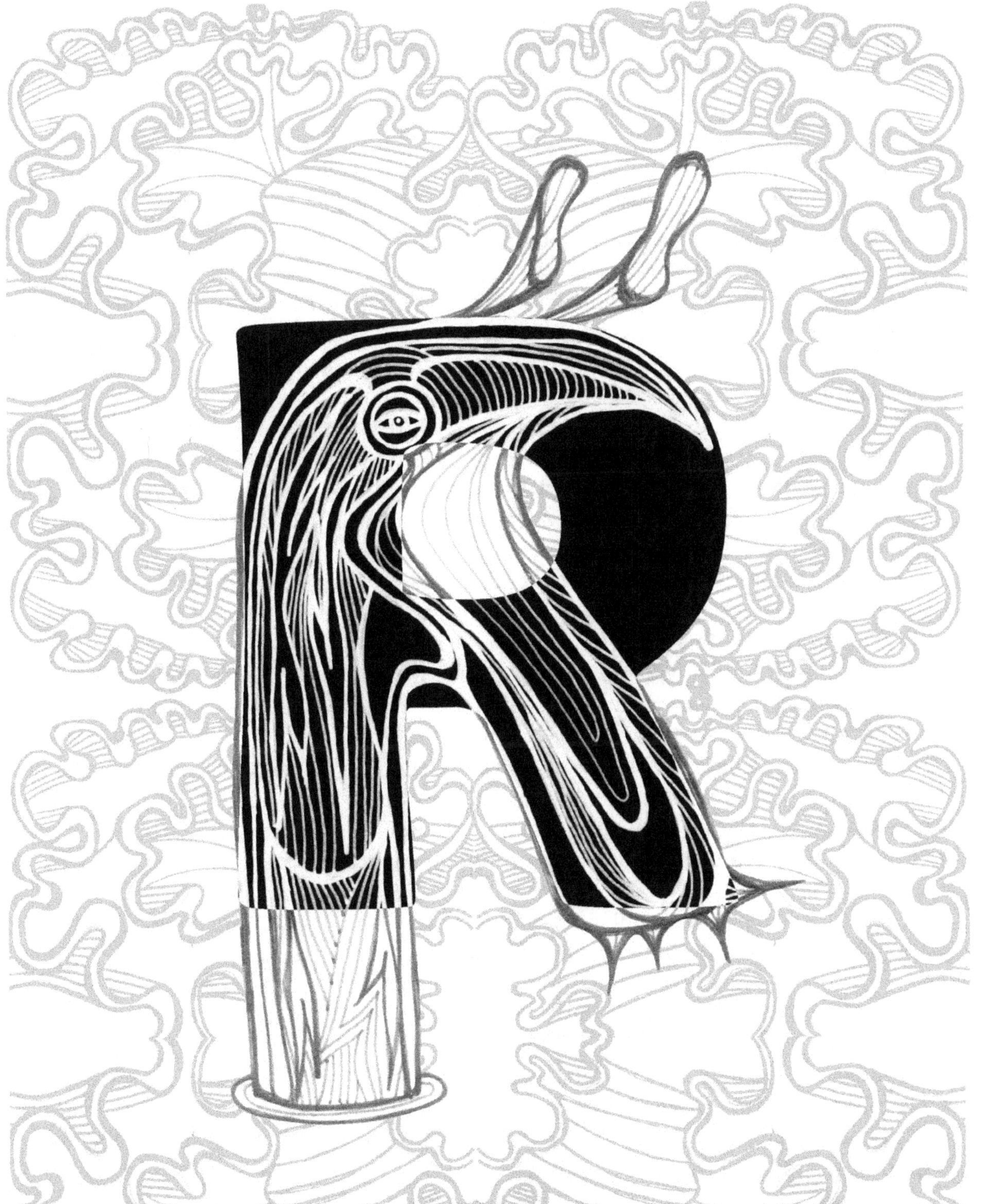

R is for Ribbon eel

R is for Ribbon Eel

Remarkable Ribbon Eel...

* Ribbon eels are one of the most flamboyant and easily recognised Morays. They have very long, flattened, brightly coloured bodies.

* Ribbon eels make their home in a range of underwater environments. Some species use burrows on a sand or mud bottom, some live along rocky shorelines and some seek a home in the rocks and crevices on coral reefs. They are bottom dwelling fish, rarely moving high in the water column.

* Ribbon eels tend to live in lagoons or coastal reefs throughout the Indian and Pacific Oceans, from East Africa to French Polynesia, as far north as southern Japan, and south to Australia and New Caledonia.

* Ribbon eel, or blue ribbon eel, these colourful animals are actually a species of moray eel.

* Ribbon eels start off as male and are black with a yellow dorsal fin. As they mature, the male eels turn mostly bright blue with yellow accents around the mouth and on the dorsal fin.

* Ribbon eel's male body reaches a certain length, it begins to turn yellow and will develop female parts until it is able to lay eggs. This is a sequential hermaphrodite.

* Ribbon eels are territorial fish, spending their days resting in a hole sticking their heads out and rhythmically sucking water through their mouths to keep a flow of water passing their gills for respiration.

* Ribbon eels are usually solitary, although they do sometimes share their home with another eel.

* Ribbon eels are nearly all nocturnal hunters, feeding at night when their poor eyesight is less of a handicap and their acute sense of smell comes into its own.

* Ribbon eels are often found waving its head around, this behaviour can often be seen as a threat, in fact they are very shy creatures and will only attack if provoked!

* Ribbon eels are known to stay in the same hole for months or even years.

* Ribbon eel stop eating in cativity and mostly do not last longer than a month.

• Ribbon eels grow to an overall length of approximately 1 m, and has a life span of up to twenty years. Really?!

Conservation Corner...

Ribbon eels live in coral reefs. It wasn't until recent years that scientists realized that reefs at much greater and darker depths also teem with life—and may be home to the majority of coral species. Yet even before these deep reefs have been fully explored and documented, they are being destroyed by unregulated deep-sea trawling.

Helping Humans...

A group of 1,136 scientists from 69 countries is appealing for new laws to protect deep-ocean corals and sponges, these communities appear to be as important to the biodiversity of the oceans and the sustainability of fisheries as their analogues in shallow tropical waters.

Action Stations...

Support the coral crew. Donate either your time or money to the organizations actively working to preserve and protect our reefs. Here are a few groups to get in touch with; Coral Reef Alliance, Surfrider Foundation, Reef Environmental Education Foundation, Reef Check, 50 Reefs, Project AWARE, and the Coastal Conservation League.

Be a green marine tourist, www.greenfins.net/en

S is for Squid

S is for Squid
Sensational Squid...

* Squids are cephalopods, along with Octopus, Cuttlefish and Nautilus. There are around 304 species of Squid.
* Squids have a distinct head, bilateral symmetry, a mantle, and arms.
* Squid, like cuttlefish, have eight arms arranged in pairs and two, usually longer, tentacles.
* Squids are strong swimmers and certain species can "fly" for short distances out of the water.
* Squid skin is covered in chromatophores, which enable the squid to change colour to suit its surroundings, making it practically invisible. The underside is also almost always lighter than the topside, to provide camouflage from both prey and predator.
* Squids have a siphon at the front of the mantle cavity, which the squid uses for locomotion via precise jet propulsion. In this form of locomotion, water is sucked into the mantle cavity and expelled out of the siphon in a fast, strong jet.
* Squids exhibit relatively high intelligence among invertebrates. For example, groups of Humboldt squid hunt cooperatively, using active communication.
* Squids are believed to be the fastest of all invertebrates in the world.
* Squids have the is the largest invertebrate in the world in their family, the Giant Squid, about 14m long!
* Squid eyes, on either side of the head, each contain a hard lens. Giant Squid have eyeballs that are the same size as a basketball.
* Squid only have one predator other than humans, Sperm Whales, captured whales often have indigestible Squid beaks in their stomachs.
* Squid have three hearts. Two branchial hearts feed the gills, each surrounding the larger systemic heart that pumps blood around the body.
* Squid are able to glow in the dark, this is due to them having bioluminescent organs. Sexy!

Conservation Corner...

Squid live in the deep sea. Deep below the Ocean's surface is a mysterious world that takes up 95% of Earth's living space. In 2004, Japanese researchers took the first images of a live Giant Squid in its natural habitat, and in July 2012, a live adult was first filmed in its natural habitat.

Helping Humans...

Practically every deep sea expedition provides something new, interesting, and important to learn about. This single collection from a suction sampler includes several different types of new deep coral.

Action Stations...

Join local efforts to protect the Oceans. Combine efforts with organisations working in your area. Here are a few groups who may have projects near you: 350. org, Citizens Climate Lobby, Environment America, Environmental Defense Fund, League of Conservation Voters, National Wildlife Federation, The Nature Conservancy, and Sierra Club's Ready for 100 campaign, Reef World Foundation.

T is for Turtle

T is for Turtle

* Turtles are air-breathing reptiles with streamlined bodies and large flippers. They are well adapted to life in the ocean and inhabit tropical and subtropical Ocean waters around the world.
* Turtles cover vast distances across the world's Oceans, filling a vital role in the balance of marine habitats.
* Turtles live all over our Ocean waters, from the shallow seagrass beds of the Indian Ocean, to the reefs of the Coral Triangle, and the sandy beaches of the Eastern Pacific.
* Turtles migrate long distances to feed, often crossing entire Oceans. Some loggerheads nest in Japan and migrate to Baja California Sur, Mexico to forage before returning home again.
* Turtles have been on Earth for more than 100 million years — even surviving the dinosaurs when they became extinct 65 million years ago.
* Turtles often drown when caught in fishing gear, both nets and long lines. Coastal development can destroy important nesting sites, impact coral reefs, and artificial light from houses and other buildings attracts hatchlings away from the Ocean.
* Turtles spend their entire lives at sea, except when adult females come ashore to lay eggs every 2 to 5 years.
* Turtles have a hard shell that protects them like a shield, this upper shell is called a 'carapace', and a lower shell called a 'plastron'.
* Turtles can hide their heads inside their shells when attacked by predators.
* Turtle size varies greatly, depending upon species — from the small Kemp's ridley, which weighs between 80–100 pounds, to the enormous leatherback, which can weigh more than 1,000 pounds.
* Turtle hatchlings merge after 60days from their sandy nests and make their way to the Ocean — attracted to the distant horizon.
* Turtles spend their first few years in the open oceans as juveniles, eventually moving to protected bays, estuaries, and other nearshore waters as adults.
* Turtles are ectotherms (cold blooded) meaning that their internal temperature varies according to the ambient environment. However, because of their high metabolic rate, leatherback sea turtles have a body temperature that is noticeably higher than that of the surrounding water.
* Turtles are classified as amniotes, along with other reptiles, birds, and mammals. Like other amniotes, turtles breathe air and do not lay eggs underwater, although many species live in or around water.
* Turtles are caught each year as by catch, 4950 by Indonesian long line vessels alone.
* Turtle temperature determines if the egg will develop into a male or female, lower temperatures lead to a male while higher temperatures lead to a female. Climate change and global warming could skew sex ratios, resulting in more females.

* Turtle species, Eastern Pacific leatherbacks, have declined by over 90% in the last 30 years.

* Turtles lay eggs in the sand and leave them to hatch on their own. The young turtles make their way to the top of the sand and scramble to the water while trying to avoid predators, this was the most dangerous part of their life, until human threats.
* Turtles feed on jellyfish, the Leatherback especially as its main food, plastic bags in the water look like jellyfish, many turtles die by trying to digest plastic bags.
* Turtle have 7 species ; Green, Hawksbill, Loggerhead, Leatherback, Flatback, Olive Ridley, Kemp's Ridley . ALL 7 of them are classified as "Vulnerable, Endangered and Critically Endangered " in the Red List of the International Union for Conservation of Nature. Terrible.

Conservation Corner... Human

activities have tipped the scales against the survival of these ancient mariners. Nearly all species of sea turtle are classified as "Endangered". Slaughtered for their eggs, meat, skin and shells, Turtles suffer from poaching and over-exploitation. They also face habitat destruction and accidental capture in fishing gear. Climate change has an impact on turtle nesting sites. It alters sand temperatures, which then affects the sex of hatchlings.

Helping Humans... Many conservation

groups including WWF are committed to stop the decline of Turtles and work for the recovery of the species. Working to secure environments in which both Turtles, and the people that depend upon them, can survive into the future.
www.worldwildlife.org/species/sea-turtle

Action Stations... Support Sea Turtle eco

tourism, particularly when it benefits local communities. Respect Turtle Territory, don't touch or chase them, it stresses them out. This can lead to exhaustion and death and it may scare them away which damages eco tourism for locals.

U is for Unicorn fish

U is for Unicorn fish

Unbelievable Unicorn fish...

* Unicorn fish has a very human feature - an unusually large nose, which is called its horn, which is where it gets its name!

*   Unicorn fish horn is between the eyes. It begins growing when a young fish reaches about 13 cm in length, and tends to be a little bigger on males.

* Unicorn fish do not use its horn for defence, but rather its sharp tail spines. Biologists are unsure of the purpose of the horn.

* Unicorn fish's mouth is perfectly designed to carefully remove the algae from coral while leaving the coral intact.

* Unicorn fish primarily live around coral reefs and eat mostly algae, lush macro algae like Sargassum, or zooplankton floating in the water column.

* Unicorn fish has the amazing ability to change its colour almost instantly depending on its environment and its mood.

* Unicorn fish are cousins to the surgeon fish and tangs, this family share the pair of sharp spikes on the caudal peduncle (where the tail meets the body). These "scalpel-sharp" weapons are the source of the name surgeon fish.

* Unicorn fish use their sharp spines to defend against potential predators, as well as to fight off other herbivores competing for tasty algae.

* Unicorn like eating the poo of other fish! Some like to wait beneath a school of larger fish and feed on their poo waste. Unusual!

Conservation Corner...

Plastic never completely breaks down, it ends up as small micro beads in algae such as sargassum, Unicorn fish food. According to the Container Recycling Institute, 100.7 billion plastic beverage bottles were sold in the U.S. in 2014, or 315 bottles per person. 57% of those units were plastic water bottles: 57.3 billion sold in 2014. This is up from 3.8 billion plastic water bottles sold in 1996.

Helping Humans...

Invest in a life long bottle, eg: Eco Bottle. Benefits Of The Eco Bottle, Made from 100% recycled materials, helps to reduce your carbon footprint, Fully customisable (make your own brand), Bisphenol A – Free, vegetable inks are used for prints, life long guarantee. www.eco-bottles.co.uk

Action Stations...

Reduce plastic use, in the US alone; Disposal razors, 2 billion thrown away and 27.4 billion disposable nappies thrown away every year.

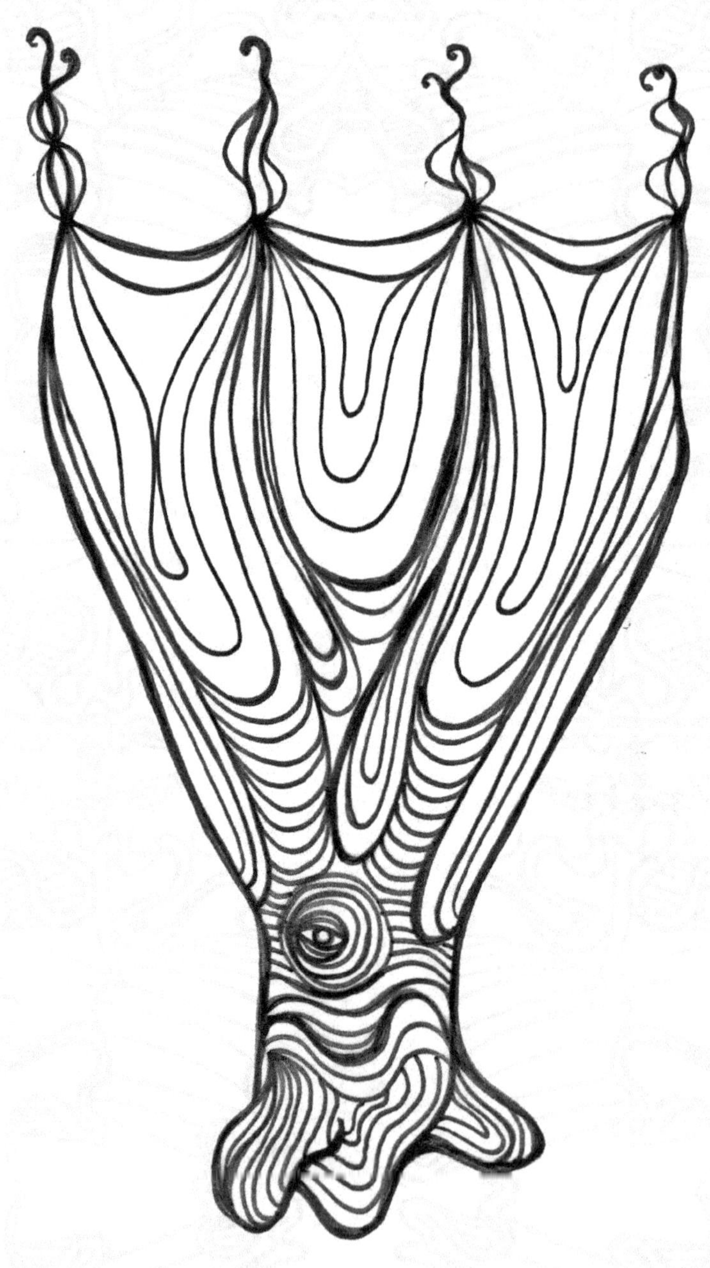

V is for
Vampire squid

V is for Vampire Squid

Victorious Vampire Squid...

*   Vampire squid's velvety jet-black to pale reddish colour, red eyes and the long arms that flow like a black cape is why this squid is called vampire!

*   Vampire squid is an extreme example of a deep-sea cephalopod, thought to reside at aphotic (lightless) depths from 600 to 900 metres (2,000 to 3,000 ft) or more!

*   Vampire squid can reach a maximum total length around 30cm.

*   Vampire squid has a webbing of skin connects its eight arms, each lined with rows of fleshy spines or cirri; the inner side of this "cloak" is black.

*   Vampire Squid mature adults have a pair of small fins projecting from the lateral sides of the mantle. These fins serve as the adult's primary means of propulsion, they can "fly" through the water by flapping their fins.

*   Vampire squid slow down their metabolism to a very low rate, this is how they are able to live in the very cold waters.

*   Vampire squid is able to live and breathe normally in the OMZ (Oxygen Minimum Zone) at oxygen saturations as low as 3%; an ability that no other cephalopod, and few other animals, possess.

*   Vampire squid maintain agility and buoyancy with little effort because of sophisticated statocysts (balancing organs akin to a humans inner ear).

*   Vampire squid can turn themselves inside out to fend off predators!

*   Vampire squid are almost entirely covered in light-producing organs called photophores, capable of producing disorienting flashes of light ranging in duration from fractions of a second to several minutes!

*   Vampire squid doesn't use ink to fend off predators it shoots out sticky mucus, which can glow in the dark for almost 10 minutes, further confusing their predators and giving the squid time to hide. Villainous!

Conservation Corner...

Over-fishing, pollution and the advent of deep sea mining pose new challenges to a previously untouched world. A habitat less well known than the surface of the Moon, most of the deep sea remains unexplored. In recent years advances in submarine technology have given us a better understanding of this environment, with new species revealed on almost every dive. Species that scientists once thought could avoid the worst impact of the sea's exploitation have recently been found to be at risk from industrial pollutants. In February this year, scientists exploring the world's deepest marine trench, the Mariana Trench, discovered extremely high levels of toxins at depths of more than 10,000 metres. Their submersible captured crustaceans that were found to carry toxic chemicals at 50 times the concentration typically found in crabs from China's most polluted rivers.

The pollutants in question were polychlorinated biphenyls, or PCBs, the industrial compounds blamed for causing severe defects in the world's marine mammals.

Helping Humans...

Individual corals could produce chemicals potentially useful for treating high blood pressure, cancer, and chronic pain. Unlike the world's rainforests, these unknown formations could be lost or damaged without anyone ever having noticed they were there.

Action Stations...

The Deep Sea Conservation Coalition (DSCC) is an alliance of over 70 international organizations working to promote the conservation of deep sea biodiversity. Follow www.savethedeepsea.blogspot.co.uk

W is for Wobbegong

W is for Wobbegong
Wonderful Wobbegong...

* Wobbegong is the common name given to the 12 species of carpet sharks. They earn this name because they are bottom-dwelling sharks, staying on the Ocean floor.
* Wobbegongs are found in shallow temperate and tropical waters of the Western Pacific Ocean and eastern Indian Ocean, chiefly around Australia and Indonesia.
* Wobbegong's name comes from the language of the Australian Aborigines it means "shaggy beard".
* Wobbegongs can be as long as 3m, this species is known as the spotted Wobbegong.
* Wobbegongs have greenish or brownish skin, which is covered in a unique pattern of bold markings, this keeps them camouflaged against the sand, hiding them from larger fish and marine mammals who could try to eat them. Unfortunately, sometimes they are so well-hidden that people end up stepping on them, resulting in nasty bites.
* Wobbegongs are nocturnal, sleeping during the day and hunting at night.
* Wobbegong sharks do not need to keep moving in order to breathe, like the Great White Shark does.
* Wobbegongs are hunters, but since they are quite lazy, instead of actively looking for food or chasing after prey, they wait for prey to come close to them and then attack in ambush.
* Wobbegongs, along with all Shark populations face the threat of extinction in every part of the world primarily due to overfishing driven by the high demand for Shark fins. Additional include by-catch, where Sharks are killed when other seafood is being targeted, recreational fishing, Sharks being used for ingredients in cosmetics or health supplements, destruction of habitat and more.
* Wobbegongs are important; Divers, when choosing a dive destination, rank Sharks and Mantas as the #1 attraction – ranking them higher than healthy coral reefs or Turtles – making them a crucial part of the economy in some parts of the world. Add to that the fact that Sharks, as apex predators, are vital to maintaining the balance of our Ocean ecosystems and you begin to understand the true value of sharks. Wow!

Conservation Corner...

The Raja Ampat Shark and Ray Sanctuary was established in November 2010 in a part of Eastern Indonesia in response to an initiative undertaken by Misool Eco Resort and Shark Savers. Misool Eco Resort established a protected no-take zone in the Southern part of Raja Ampat around its resort in 2005 and expanded it in 2010. This Marine Conservation Area ("MCA") was created in cooperation with the local villages that own the rights to the reefs. A team of rangers, comprised of local villagers, patrols the MCA in conjunction with Misool Eco Resort. Misool Eco Resort MCA sits within the larger Raja Ampat Shark and Ray Sanctuary. The Sanctuary bans the fishing of Sharks, Rays, Turtles, Dugongs, and also bans destructive fishing practices such as dynamiting, poison, purse seine, and other methods.

Helping Humans...

Misool Eco Resort and its local Ranger Patrol have been highly successful in improving the fish biomass in the area and bringing an end to previously rampant destructive fishing practices. Noticing a dramatic increase in the number of Snappers, Groupers, and Napoleon wrasse on these reefs since the implementation of their innovative community agreement for a no-fishing zone in the area. Also more Sharks within the MCA boundaries than in the preceding 6 years' combined.

Action Stations...

Follow and support Shark Savers through their many Shark and Ray conservation projects www.sharksavers.org/en/home

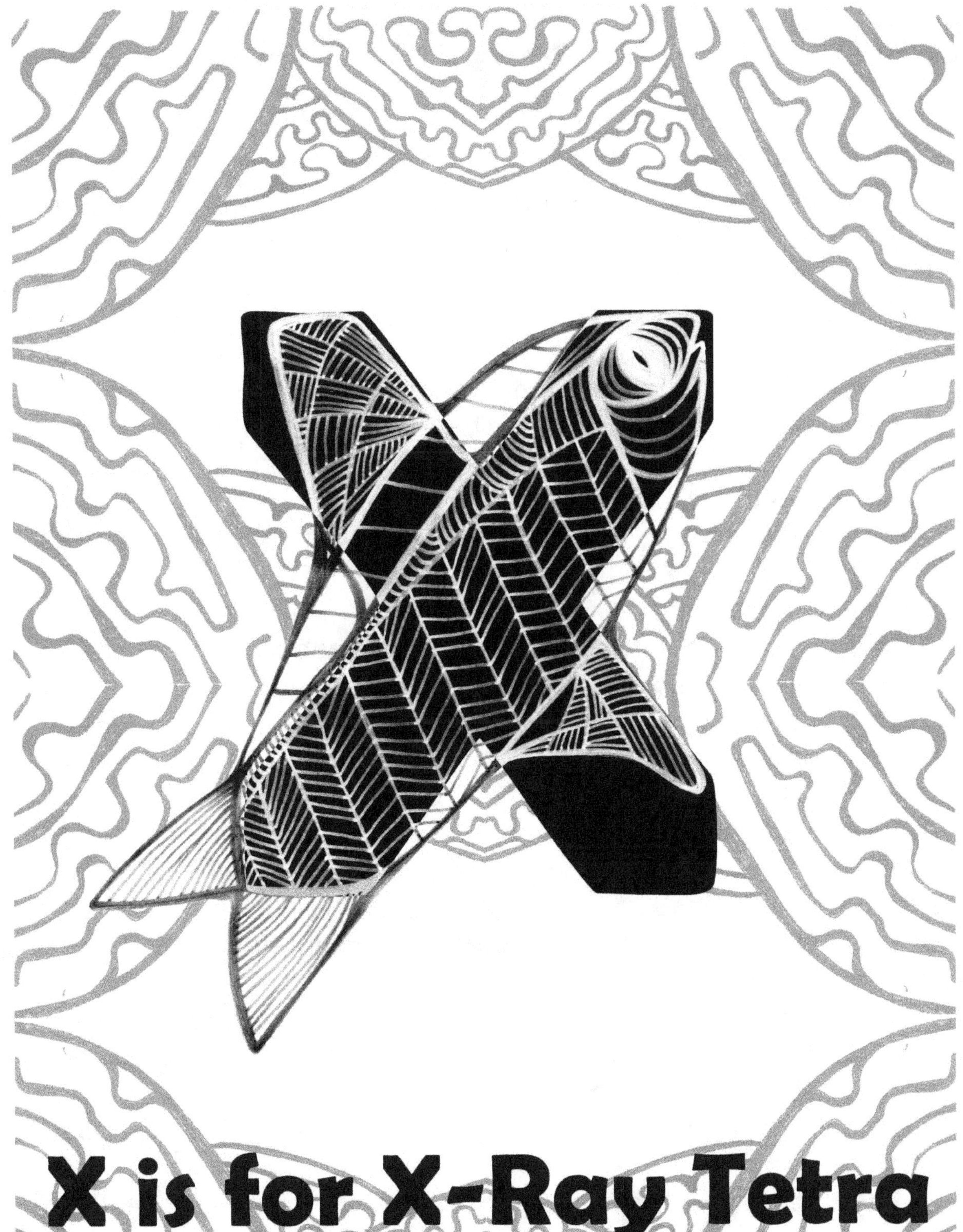

X is for X-Ray Tetra

X is for X-Ray Tetra

Xtraordinary X-Ray Tetra...

* X-Ray Tetra is a small species of schooling fish that is naturally found in the Amazon River's coastal waters in South America.
* X-Ray Tetra are one of the few animals that are transparent or translucent, hence their name.
* X-Ray Tetras have special skin, this helps in camouflage by allowing them to blend in against their environment.
* X-Ray Tetra is also known as the Golden Pristella Tetra and the Water Goldfinch due to the faint golden colouration of their translucent skin.
* X-Ray Tetras can be found in both salt and fresh waters, both acidic and alkaline, and both clear and brackish, most can only survive in one of all three variables.
* X-Ray Tetras are a schooling sepcies of fish inhabiting the region between the bottom and middle of the water.
* X-Ray Tetra are peaceful and tolerant of the other species that they share their habitats with.
* X-Ray Tetra is one of nearly 100 other Tetra species.
* X-Ray Tetra primarily hunt worms, insects and small crustaceans that live close to the river bed and their fry tend to feed on insects larvae.
* X-Ray Tetra have weberian apparatus (the bony structure) in their body . They can transmit sound waves through their vertebrate, then receive transmissions by the swim bladder and and take it to the inner ear, this ability means that they have excellent hearing.
* X-Ray Tetra females are usually bigger than males, this is called sexual dimorphism.
* X-Ray Tetras are small about 5cm and they live in large groups. Xtra!

Conservation Corner... X-Ray Tetra

populations are thought to be under threat from the rising levels of pollution in the water and habitat loss. Increasing industry in the Amazon Basin means that there has been an increase in the levels of pollution in the water a decrease in water quality, leading to population declines in certain areas. Soy farming and pollution run-off contribute to this problem. Market demands for cheap animal based foods, made out of livestock raised on soy (as it is inexpensive to grow), and by increased meat consumption in countries such as China. Cheap meat has become a way of life in much of Europe, but the full price is being paid across Latin America as vast soya plantations and their attendant chemicals lead to poisoning the Amazon basin.

Helping Humans... The Amazon is an incredible

place. It's ecosystem stores 17% of the world's carbon which helps regulate the Earth's temperature.

Action Stations... Do some research, watch;

Killing Fields: the battle to feed factory farms – produced by a coalition of pressure groups including Friends of the Earth, Food and Water Watch and with European coordination by Via Campesina. Read food labels to seek out soy free alternatives.

Y is for
Yellow sea slug

Y is for Yellow Sea Cucumber

Yes! Yellow Sea Cucumber facts;

* Yellow sea cucumbers are named after their resemblance to cucumber's!
* Yellow sea cucumbers can live up to 10 years old.
* Yellow sea cucumbers can grow up to 6ft!
* Yellow sea cucumbers are echinoderms—like starfish and sea urchins.
* Yellow sea cucumbers are among some 1,250 known species, most of which are shaped like soft-bodied cucumbers.
* Yellow sea cucumbers are Ocean dwellers, though some inhabit the shallows and deep ocean. They live on, or near, the Ocean floor, sometimes partially buried beneath it.
* Yellow sea cucumbers feed on tiny particles like algae, minute aquatic animals, or waste materials, which they gather in with 8 to 30 tube feet that look like tentacles surrounding their mouths.
* Yellow sea cucumbers break down these particles into even smaller pieces, which become fodder for bacteria, and thus recycle them back into the Ocean ecosystem. Earthworms perform a similar function in terrestrial ecosystems.
* Yellow sea cucumbers, particularly their eggs and young larvae, are prey for fish and other marine animals. They are eaten by humans, especially in Asia.
* Yellow sea cucumbers discharge sticky threads to ensnare their enemies.
* Yellow sea cucumbers can breed sexually or asexually. Sexual reproduction is more typical, the animals release both eggs and sperm into the water and fertilization occurs when they meet.
* Yellow sea cucumbers live in large herds in parts of the deep ocean, grazing on the microscopic bounty of marine waters.
* Yellow sea cucumbers can mutilate their own bodies as a defense mechanism. They violently contract their muscles and jettison some of their internal organs out of their anus. The missing body parts are quickly regenerated. Yuk!

Conservation Corner...

Sea cucumbers saving lives! As fish stocks dwindle, communities that rely on the Ocean for their livelihood are struggling to survive. Blue venture marine conservation charity in Madagascar is challenging the accepted wisdom of marine conservation with a combination of sea cucumber farming and family planning.

Helping Humans...

Sea cucumbers serve a useful role in the marine ecosystem as they help recycle nutrients, breaking down detritus and other organic matter after which bacteria can continue the degradation process.

Action Stations...

Blue Ventures' most pioneering projects include; the world's first community-based sea cucumber farm. Working with the University of Toliara's institute of marine science, the local seafood exporter Copefrito and Indian Ocean Trepang (IOT), a local company that breeds sea cucumbers, Blue Ventures has spent £1.2 million on the project since 2008, buying juveniles, building the pens and providing technical advice.
www.blueventures.org

Z is for Zebra crab

Z is for Zebra Crab

* Zebra crabs have Zebra like patterns, which is where it gets its name, this also acts as good camouflage against predators.

* Zebra crabs live on their own or in pairs.

* Zebra crabs are covered with a thick exoskeleton and have a single pair of claws.

* Zebra crabs are considered true crabs, they have a short abdomen, 4 walking legs and a pair of clawed arms at the front.

* Zebra crabs are about 2 cm long, they live 5-15 m deep in the Ocean.

* Zebra crabs have internal fertilization and mate belly-to-belly.

* Zebra crabs can store the sperm for a long time before using it to fertilize their eggs. When fertilization has taken place, the eggs are released onto the female's abdomen, below the tail flap, secured with a sticky material. In this location, they are protected during embryonic development. Females carrying eggs are called "berried" since the eggs resemble round berries.

* Zebra crabs lives on the surface of the fire urchin. Fire urchins are venomous to others but not the Zebra crab.

* Zebra crabs live on and eat the Fire Urchins, they eat plankton caught in the spines of the urchin.

* Zebra crabs have a "Commensalism" relationship with the urchin, meaning the crab benefits from the relationship but the urchin is left unaffected. Zesty!

Conservation Corner...

Excess CO2 dissolves into the Ocean and is converted to corrosive carbonic acid, a process known as "Ocean acidification". At the same time, the CO2 also supplies carbon that combines with calcium already dissolved in seawater to provide the main ingredient for shells, calcium carbonate (CaCO3), the same material found in chalk and limestone. Under experimental CO2 conditions, the shells of clams, oysters, and some snails and urchins partially dissolved. But other species seemed as if they would not be harmed, and crustaceans, such as lobsters, crabs, and prawns, appeared to increase their shell-building. It is unknown how this will affect the Zebra crab or the Urchin, the Zebra Crab may lose the Urchin or vice versa, it will undoubtable change the marine eco system.

Helping Humans...

Since the beginning of the industrial revolution, the release of carbon dioxide (CO2) from humankind's industrial and agricultural activities has increased the amount of CO2 in the atmosphere. The Ocean absorbs about a quarter of the CO2 we release into the atmosphere every year, so as atmospheric CO2 levels increase, so do the levels in the Ocean. Initially, many scientists focused on the benefits of the Ocean removing this greenhouse gas from the atmosphere. However, decades of Ocean observations now show that there is also a downside — the CO2 absorbed by the ocean is changing the chemistry of the seawater, a process called Ocean acidification.

Action Stations...

Education and Action! Living sustainably- www.permaculture.org.uk

Profits from the sales of ABC in the SEA go to
Atelier Aquatic Community Interest Company
Atelieraquatic.org

www.ingramcontent.com/pod-product-compliance
Lightning Source LLC
Chambersburg PA
CBHW081521250726
48659CB00009B/2887